PASTA

Sunset Creative Cooking Library

By the Editors of Sunset Books

SUNSET BOOKS
President & Publisher: Susan J. Maruyama
Director, Finance & Business Affairs: Gary Loebner
**Director, Manufacturing
& Sales Service:** Lorinda Reichert

SUNSET PUBLISHING CORPORATION
Chairman: Robert L. Miller
President/Chief Executive Officer: Robin Wolaner
Chief Financial Officer: James E. Mitchell
Circulation Director: Robert I. Gursha
Editor, Sunset Magazine: William R. Marken

All the recipes in this book were developed and tested in the Sunset test kitchens. For information about any Sunset Book please call 1-800-634-3095.

The nutritional data provided for each recipe is for a single serving, based on the number of servings and the amount of each ingredient. If a range is given for the number of servings and/or the amount of an ingredient, the analysis is based on the average of the figures given. The nutritional analysis does not include optional ingredients or those for which no specific amount is stated. If an ingredient is listed with a substitution, the data was calculated using the first choice.

Nutritional analysis of recipes: Hill Nutrition Associates, Inc. of Florida.

Sunset Creative Cooking Library
was produced by St. Remy Press

Publisher: Kenneth Winchester
President: Pierre Léveillé
Managing Editor: Carolyn Jackson
Senior Editor: Elizabeth Cameron
Managing Art Director: Diane Denoncourt
Administrator: Natalie Watanabe
Production Manager: Michelle Turbide
System Coordinator: Jean-Luc Roy
Proofreader: Garet Markvoort
Indexer: Christine Jacobs

COVER: *Linguine with Prosciutto & Olives (page 17)*

PHOTOGRAPHY
Robert Chartier: 4-5, 18, 26, 35, 42, 50, 59, 60;
Glenn Christiansen: 28, 44; Peter Christiansen: 6;
Kevin Sanchez: 12, 14, 22; Darrow M. Watt: 38;
Tom Wyatt: 9, 10, 11, 30, 36, 52; Nikolay Zurek: 16,
20, 24, 46, 48, 54, 56, 62.

PHOTO STYLING
Susan Massey-Weil: 12, 14, 16, 20, 22, 24, 30, 44,
46, 48, 54, 56, 62; Cynthia Scheer: 36, 52, 56.

ISBN 0-376-00902-0
Library of Congress Catalog Card Number 94-67312
Printed in the United States

✸ printed on recycled paper.

Table of Contents

Pasta Basics
4

Light & Healthy
12

Robust Meals
30

Festive Fare
46

Index
64

Different Pasta Shapes

What's your favorite pasta shape—long strands of spaghetti? Bouncy spirals of fusilli? Tender ribbons of fettuccine? This gallery of dried pasta displays some of the many different shapes, sizes, and colors of this versatile and imaginative ingredient. You can often judge the size from the Italian suffix: "oni" means large; "elle," "ine," and "ini," all diminuitives, mean the pasta is small.

Linguine

Macaroni

Conchiglie

Lasagne

Farfalle

Perciatelli

Fusilli

Capelli
d'angeli

Penne

Spaghetti

Pasta with Pizzazz

Market-fresh ingredients, Parmesan cheese, and Italian olive oil play starring roles in many pasta dishes.

Touring Italy's many kitchens unlocks a treasure trove of good food. Like a gallery director selecting the best of the collection for display, we've chosen a tantalizing array of Italy's prize culinary works of art. You'll find recipes for relaxed family meals as well as elaborate dishes for entertaining.

Whatever you choose to prepare, shopping for ingredients presents few challenges if you live in a metropolitan area. A large supermarket will provide all you need for most of the recipes in this book, while a good Italian delicatessen can offer the rest, including a variety of fresh pasta, olives, Italian cheeses and sausages. So stock your kitchen with such necessities as olive oil, garlic, Parmesan cheese, basil, and oregano—and let your culinary cooking tour begin.

Cooking Pasta Perfectly

The ideal state for cooked pasta is summed up in the Italian phrase *al dente*—to the tooth, or tender but still firm. To achieve such perfectly cooked pasta, use plenty of water; pasta in an abundance of rapidly boiling water is unlikely to stick to itself or to the pan. Be sure to choose a pan that can comfortably hold the amount of boiling water you will need.

How much pasta to cook? As a general rule, 2 ounces dry pasta make about 1 cup cooked pasta, or 1 serving. Spaghetti and macaroni products approximately double in volume upon cooking. Fresh pasta is moister than the dry pasta, so you'll need a greater weight per serving—3 to 3½ ounces make 1 cup (about 1 serving). A kitchen scale allows you to weigh out pasta accurately, but you can measure by eye—note the number of ounces in a package and estimate the proportion of the package needed.

For each 8 ounces dry pasta, bring 3 quarts water to a rapid boil. Add 1 tablespoon salt, if desired (for more pasta, increase the amount of water only). Add the pasta to the boiling water. When you cook pasta that's longer than the pan is deep, hold the pasta by one end, then gently push the other end into the boiling water until the strands soften enough to submerge. Stir only if the pasta needs to be separated. Keep the water boiling continuously and cook the pasta, uncovered, according to the cooking time specified in the recipe.

Cooking time varies with the pasta's size and shape—the thinner and moister the pasta, the shorter the cooking time. Our recipes specify the time it took our testers. But because one manufacturer's spaghetti may cook faster than another's, it's always wise to check the cooking time specified on the package. A quick, reliable test for doneness is simply to lift a piece or strand from the pan and quickly bite into it; if it's al dente, it's done. Pasta that breaks easily against the side of the pan when prodded with a spoon has probably been cooked too long.

If the pasta is destined for a baked casserole, shorten the cooking time by a few minutes to allow for additional cooking in the oven.

As soon as the pasta is al dente, drain it quickly and continue according to the recipe. Rinse cooked pasta only if you're going to use it in a salad or need to cool lasagne noodles in order to handle them. Pasta that will be served at once should not be rinsed; to keep it as hot as possible, have a warm platter or plates—and your family or guests—ready and waiting. (Don't worry about excess water clinging to the drained pasta, it will blend in with the sauce.)

Making Pasta at Home

Finding a place to set long strips of thinly rolled dough is one of the first steps you need to plan. You'll need space for about 16 feet of 4-inch-wide dough strips. Avoid laminated plastic surfaces; dough tends to sweat and stick to them. Once you've selected your space, cover it with tea towels or sheets; flour the cloths lightly. Besides a space for dough strips you need a work surface—kitchen counter or table—that is a comfortable height for mixing and kneading dough.

Equipment is fairly simple. You can mix the dough in a large bowl or directly on your work surface. To mix the dough, you need a fork for stirring, plus a measuring cup and measuring spoons. To roll the dough out, you can use a pasta machine or rely on an arm-powered rolling pin.

Four Pasta Recipes

All-Purpose Pasta
2 cups all-purpose flour
2 large eggs
3 to 6 Tbsp. water
(Additional flour for kneading, rolling, and cutting)

Whole Wheat Pasta
1¾ cups whole wheat flour
¼ cup toasted wheat germ
2 large eggs
3 to 6 Tbsp. water
(Additional flour for kneading, rolling, and cutting)

Spinach Pasta
2 cups all-purpose flour
2 large eggs
½ package (10-oz. size) frozen spinach, cooked, cooled, chopped, and squeezed dry
(Additional flour for kneading, rolling, and cutting)

Rosy Pasta
2 cups all-purpose flour
2 large eggs
3 Tbsp. strained carrots, beets for babies, or tomato paste
(Additional flour for kneading, rolling, and cutting)

1. Mound flour (and wheat germ, if preparing Whole Wheat Pasta) on a work surface or in a large bowl. Make a deep well and break eggs into well.

2. Use a fork to beat eggs lightly. For All-Purpose and Whole Wheat Pasta, mix in 2 tablespoons of water; for Spinach and Rosy Pasta, stir in wet ingredients (spinach, carrots, beets, or tomato paste). Using a circular motion, draw flour from sides.

3. For All-Purpose and Whole Wheat Pasta, add 1 tablespoon of water and continue mixing. Add a little more water, if necessary, to moisten all the flour. If Spinach or Rosy Pasta dough is crumbly, add a few drops of water.

4. Use your hands to finish mixing when dough becomes too stiff to work with the fork. Push and pat dough into the shape of a ball.

5. Fold and press dough to help flour absorb the liquid. If dough is sticky, sprinkle on a little flour; if dough is crumbly, drizzle on a few drops of water.

6. Clean and flour work surface. Knead, rotating dough a quarter turn each time until it's smooth, elastic, and no longer sticky. Cover; let rest 20 minutes.

Cutting Pasta Two Ways

Once you've kneaded the dough and let it rest, you're ready to roll it out. Keeping unrolled portions of dough covered, roll out a fourth of the dough into a rectangle about $1/16$ inch thick with a rolling pin. If dough is sticky, turn and flour both sides as you roll. Transfer rolled strip to a lightly floured surface or cloth and let stand, uncovered, while you roll remaining portions. Let each rolled-out strip dry for 5 to 10 minutes before cutting it. Be careful—it's easy to dry the strips too long; check that they don't become brittle. Turn the strips over to dry briefly on both sides.

The following directions for cutting pasta by machine apply to both manual and electric machines. If you are cutting pasta by hand, don't worry about cutting them precisely $1/4$ or $1/8$ inch wide. Whatever shape you cut, the Italians probably have a name for it—including *maltagliati*, which literally means "miscut" pasta.

By hand

1. To roll by hand, flour the work surface and roll out $1/4$ of the dough at a time. Roll it into a rectangle about $1/16$ inch thick. If dough is sticky, turn and flour both sides as you roll.

2. Let rolled-out strips dry for a few minutes until they're like chamois cloth. Flour strip and roll up, jelly roll fashion, from the narrow end. Cut into slices as wide as you want the noodles.

By machine

1. Cut dough into 4 portions. Keeping unrolled portions covered, flatten $1/4$ of the dough slightly, flour it, then feed through widest roller setting.

What to do when...

... dough gets stuck in the roller or blades?

Some pasta machines' rollers can be reversed. If the dough is not too tangled, sprinkle stuck dough with flour and try reversing the rollers. Otherwise, cut off unstuck portion of dough, take a stiff brush, and clean out the rollers or blades. Do not use water—most pasta machines will rust if cleaned with water.

To prevent further sticking, flour the dough strip on both sides each time it is rolled; also flour the rollers. Hold the dough straight while you feed it into the rollers. If necessary, cut the strip in half for easier handling.

If you've ruined a strip, don't worry; it's easy to repair. Just fold it up, reset the rollers at the widest position, and start rolling out the strip all over again.

... dough comes out in a skinny strip?

To stretch dough to the full width of the rollers, set the pasta machine rollers in the widest position, fold dough into thirds, then feed the wider, folded side through the rollers. Repeat until the dough reaches the full width of the rollers.

2. *Fold dough into thirds and feed again through widest roller setting. Flour both sides of dough if it's sticky. Repeat folding and rolling until dough is smooth and pliable.*

3. *Set rollers one notch closer together and feed dough through. Repeat the rolling, setting rollers closer each time, until strip is as thin as you want it. Repeat with remaining dough.*

4. *Let rolled-out strips dry for a few minutes until they're like chamois cloth. Attach cutting blades to pasta machine and feed each strip through. Lightly flour the cut pasta.*

LIGHT & HEALTHY

Farfalle with Fresh Tomatoes & Basil

*Typical of the simple goodness of Italian food,
this dish can be tossed together in minutes, but it's full
of lasting flavor and nutrition.*

PER SERVING: *386 calories, 13 g protein, 73 g carbohydrates, 5 g total fat, 0 mg cholesterol, 18 mg sodium*

PREPARATION TIME: *10 min.*
COOKING TIME: *7 to 9 min.*

*12 oz. farfalle or other
   dry pasta shape*
1 Tbsp. olive oil
*2 cloves garlic, minced
   or pressed*
*1 lb. ripe pear-shaped toma-
   toes, coarsely chopped*
*1 cup tightly packed fresh
   basil leaves, torn into
   pieces*
Coarsely ground pepper
Grated Parmesan cheese

In an 8- to 10-quart pan, cook pasta in 6 quarts boiling water until al dente (7 to 9 minutes, or according to package directions).

Meanwhile, heat oil in a large frying pan over medium heat. Add garlic and cook, stirring, for 1 minute. Add tomatoes and cook, stirring, just until tomatoes begin to soften (about 3 minutes). Remove from heat.

Drain pasta and place in a large, warm bowl or platter. Add tomato mixture and basil; toss well. Season to taste with pepper and sprinkle with Parmesan at the table.

Makes 4 servings

Pasta with
Parsley-Lemon Pesto

*The sprightly flavors
of parsley and lemon stand in for basil
in this twist on a classic pesto.*

∞

PER SERVING: *488 calories, 18 g protein, 71 g carbohydrates, 14 g total fat, 12 mg cholesterol, 291 mg sodium*

PREPARATION TIME: *10 min.*
COOKING TIME: *7 to 9 min.*

*1 lb. penne, rigatoni, or
other dry pasta shape*
1 large lemon (about 5 oz.)
*2 cups lightly packed,
chopped fresh parsley
(preferably Italian)*
2 cloves garlic
*3 oz. (about 1/4 cup)
grated Parmesan cheese*
*3 Tbsp. extra-virgin
olive oil*
Coarsely ground pepper

In an 8- to 10-quart pan, cook pasta in 6 quarts boiling water until al dente (7 to 9 minutes, or according to package directions).

Meanwhile, use a vegetable peeler to pare zest (colored part of peel) from lemon in large strips (reserve lemon for other uses). In a food processor, whirl lemon zest, parsley, garlic, and Parmesan until finely minced, scraping down sides of bowl as needed. (Or mince lemon zest, parsley, and garlic by hand; stir in cheese.)

Drain pasta and place in a large, warm bowl. Add parsley mixture and oil; toss well. Season to taste with pepper.

Makes 4 to 6 servings

Linguine with Prosciutto & Olives

The fragrance and sweet-salty flavor of premium-priced prosciutto permeate this dish—yet you need just 2 ounces of the meat to serve four.

∞

PER SERVING: 461 calories, 18 g protein, 45 g carbohydrates, 23 g total fat, 23 mg cholesterol, 1044 mg sodium

PREPARATION TIME: *15 min.*
COOKING TIME: *8 to 10 min.*

*8 oz. dry or 9 oz.
  fresh linguine*
¹/4 cup olive oil
*2 oz. thinly sliced prosciutto,
  cut into ¹/4-inch-wide strips*
*¹/2 cup thinly sliced green
  onions (including tops)*
*1 jar (3 oz.) pimento-stuffed
  olives, drained*
*1 cup cherry tomatoes,
  cut into halves*
*¹/2 to ²/3 cup grated
  Parmesan cheese*

In a 5- to 6-quart pan, cook linguine in 3 quarts boiling water until al dente (8 to 10 minutes, or according to package directions). Drain well and transfer to a warm serving bowl.

While linguine is cooking, heat oil in a medium-size frying pan over medium-high heat; add prosciutto and cook, stirring often, until lightly browned (3 to 4 minutes). Add green onions and stir just until they begin to soften. Add olives and tomatoes; shake pan often until olives are hot (about 2 minutes). Pour prosciutto mixture over linguine; using two forks, lift and mix. Sprinkle with Parmesan at the table.

Makes 4 servings

Peppery Pasta

This is the kind of pasta dish that requires boiling the pasta water before you even begin making the sauce. Despite the simple ingredients, it's a spicy favorite with Italians.

PER SERVING: *305 calories, 7 g protein, 33 g carbohydrates, 16 g total fat, 43 mg cholesterol, 231 mg sodium*

PREPARATION TIME: *3 min.*
COOKING TIME: *8 to 10 min.*

*8 oz. dry medium-
   wide noodles*
1/3 cup olive oil
*2 small, dried hot red chiles,
   each broken into 3 pieces*
*2 cloves garlic, minced
   or pressed*
1/2 tsp. salt
*1/2 cup chopped
   fresh parsley*

In a 5- to 6-quart pan, cook noodles in 3 quarts boiling water until al dente (8 to 10 minutes, or according to package directions).

Meanwhile, heat olive oil in a small pan over low heat. Add chiles and cook until they begin to brown.

Add garlic and cook for about 30 seconds more or just until limp (do not brown). Add salt and parsley and cook, stirring occasionally, for 1 minute more. Remove from heat.

Drain pasta well and transfer to a warm serving platter. Spoon hot sauce over noodles. Lift and mix gently, then serve.

Makes 4 to 6 servings

Midsummer Pasta

*Celebrate the midsummer joy of vine-ripened tomatoes
with this quick pasta dish topped with chilled,
quartered fresh tomatoes.*

∞

PER SERVING: 366 calories, 10 g protein, 60 g carbohydrates, 7 g total fat, 0 mg cholesterol, 479 mg sodium

PREPARATION TIME: *10 min.*
COOKING TIME: *15 min.*

3 Tbsp. olive oil or salad oil
2 cloves garlic, minced
   or pressed
1 large onion, chopped
3/4 tsp. salt
1/4 tsp. pepper
1/8 tsp. anise seed, crushed
1 1/2 tsp. oregano leaves
1/2 tsp. **each** dry rosemary
   and paprika
1 cup dry red wine
16 oz. dry rotelle
2 1/2 lb. (about 6 medium-
   size) tomatoes, peeled,
   seeded, and quartered
3 or 4 green onions, sliced
1/2 green pepper, seeded
   and coarsely chopped
Grated Parmesan cheese

Heat oil in a wide frying pan over medium heat. Add garlic and coarsely chopped onion and cook, stirring occasionally, until onion is limp.

Add salt, pepper, anise, oregano, rosemary, paprika, and wine.

Cover the frying pan, reduce heat, and simmer for about 15 minutes.

In an 8- to 10-quart pan, cook rotelle in 6 quarts boiling water until al dente (7 to 9 minutes, or according to package directions). Drain; then mix with warm onion-wine mixture and turn onto a large platter.

Top with tomatoes, onions, and green pepper. Sprinkle with Parmesan at the table.

Makes 6 to 8 servings

P A S T A

Pasta with Pine Nut-Butter Sauce

Three colors of fettuccine, coated with a tantalizing pine nut-butter sauce, mingle in this bright first course.

∽

PER SERVING: *552 calories, 15 g protein, 67 g carbohydrates, 26 g total fat, 136 mg cholesterol, 223 mg sodium*

PREPARATION TIME: *3 min.*
COOKING TIME: *9 min.*

1 lb. dry tricolor fettuccine
1/2 cup (1/4 lb.) butter
  or margarine
1 medium-size red bell
  pepper (about 5 oz.),
  seeded and thinly slivered
1/4 cup pine nuts

In an 8- to 10-quart pan, cook pasta in 6 quarts boiling water until al dente (7 to 9 minutes or according to package directions).

Meanwhile, melt butter in a medium-size frying pan over medium heat. Add bell pepper and cook, stirring often, until limp but not brown (4 to 6 minutes). Stir in pine nuts and cook until lightly toasted (2 to 3 minutes).

Drain pasta well and place on a warm platter. Spoon hot sauce over noodles. Lift and mix gently, then serve.

Makes 4 to 6 servings

Cool Pasta Shells
with Scallops

P A S T A

*Tender scallops, fresh basil, and broccoli flowerets
look especially festive with shell-shaped pasta in this elegant
first course or light entrée.*

∞

PER SERVING: *398 calories, 26 g protein, 47 g carbohydrates, 13 g total fat, 30 mg cholesterol, 180 mg sodium*

PREPARATION TIME: *20 min.*
COOKING TIME: *15 min.*
CHILLING TIME: *2 hr.*

*8 oz. medium-size dry
pasta shells
4 cups broccoli flowerets,
cut into bite-size pieces
1 lb. sea scallops, rinsed,
drained, and cut in half
horizontally
1/4 cup **each** lemon juice,
white wine vinegar,
and olive oil
1 tsp. **each** dry mustard
and sugar
1 clove garlic, minced
or pressed
1 cup finely chopped
fresh basil leaves
Inner leaves from 2 large
heads romaine lettuce,
rinsed and crisped*

In a 5- to 6-quart pan, cook pasta in 3 quarts boiling water until al dente (7 to 9 minutes, or according to package directions). Drain, rinse with cold water until cool, and drain again. Set aside.

In a wide frying pan, cook broccoli, covered, in 1/4 inch boiling water until tender-crisp (about 4 minutes). Drain, immerse in ice water until cool, and drain again. Set aside. In same pan, cook scallops, covered in 1/4 inch boiling water until opaque in center (about 3 minutes); cut to test. Drain; set aside.

In a large bowl, mix lemon juice, vinegar, oil, mustard, sugar, garlic, and basil. Add pasta, broccoli, and scallops; mix gently. Cover and refrigerate for at least 2 hours or until next day.

Arrange lettuce on individual plates; top with pasta mixture.

Makes 4 to 6 servings

Parsley Pesto
Grilled Vegetables & Fettuccine

*For a colorful vegetarian meal from the barbeque,
arrange savory grilled vegetables over a mound
of tender green fettuccine.*

∽

PER SERVING: *837 calories, 23 g protein, 61 g carbohydrates, 58 g total fat, 120 mg cholesterol, 517 mg sodium*

PREPARATION TIME: *10 min.*
COOKING TIME: *15 min.*

*1¹/₂ cups lightly packed
Italian parsley
1 cup Parmesan cheese
²/₃ cup olive oil
3 cloves garlic, coarsely
chopped
Salt and pepper
4 small zucchini
(10 to 12 oz. total)
2 small Japanese eggplants
(about 8 oz. total) halved
lengthwise
4 small pear-shaped
tomatoes (about 6 oz.
total), halved lengthwise
1 medium-size red onion,
unpeeled, quartered
9 oz. dry green fettuccine
¹/₂ cup whipping cream*

In a food processor or blender, whirl Italian parsley, ¾ cup Parmesan cheese, olive oil, and garlic until puréed. Season with salt and pepper; set aside.

Slice zucchini lengthwise into thin strips, leaving strips attached at stem. Brush cut surfaces of zucchinni, eggplants, tomatoes, and onion with some pesto. Cook vegetables, cut sides down, on a greased grill 4 to 6 inches above a bed of medium-hot coals, until just tender when pierced. As each vegetable is cooked, remove it from grill and keep warm.

Meanwhile, cook pasta in a large pan of boiling water, following package directions. Drain well.

In a wide frying pan, combine cream and remaining pesto; bring to a boil over high heat. Remove from heat; quickly add pasta and mix lightly, using 2 forks. Divide among 4 dinner plates. Arrange vegetables over pasta, spreading zucchini into fans. Sprinkle with Parmesan at the table.

Makes 4 servings

Green Noodles with Zucchini Sauce

*You can use any variety
of summer squash to make this garden-fresh
sauce for pasta.*

PER SERVING: *375 calories, 11 g protein, 55 g carbohydrates, 13 g total fat, 54 mg cholesterol, 810 mg sodium*

PREPARATION TIME: *10 min.*
COOKING TIME: *45 min.*

*1 large onion, chopped
1 red bell or green pepper,
  seeded and chopped
1 clove garlic, minced
  or pressed
3 Tbsp. olive oil or salad oil
1 can (about 1 lb.) Italian-
  style tomatoes
3 Tbsp. chopped parsley
1/2 tsp. **each** dry basil and
  marjoram leaves
3/4 tsp. salt
1/4 tsp. pepper
1/4 cup dry red wine
3 medium-size (about 1 lb.)
  zucchini, thinly sliced
  crosswise
8 oz. dry wide noodles
Grated Parmesan cheese*

In a large frying pan over medium-high heat, cook onion, red pepper, and garlic in oil until vegetables are limp. Add tomatoes and their liquid (break up tomatoes with a spoon), as well as parsley, basil, marjoram, salt, pepper, and wine. Stirring, bring to a boil; then reduce heat, cover, and simmer for 30 minutes. Stir in zucchini and cook, covered, until crisp-tender (5 to 7 minutes).

Cook noodles in a large pan of boiling water until al dente, following package directions. Drain noodles, then place in a serving bowl. Spoon sauce over noodles, toss gently, then serve. Sprinkle with Parmesan at the table.

Makes 4 servings

Tagliarini with Garlic Sauce

The aroma of six garlic cloves gently bubbling in olive oil leaves no doubt that this dish is for garlic lovers. But don't be deterred by all the garlic—it loses its pungency and mellows with slow cooking.

∽

PER SERVING: *320 calories, 7 g protein, 40 g carbohydrates, 15 g total fat, 00 mg cholesterol, 496 mg sodium*

PREPARATION TIME: *10 min.*
COOKING TIME: *20 min.*

2 large tomatoes or
  1 can (about 1 lb.)
  Italian-style tomatoes
¹/₄ cup water
1 tsp. dry basil
³/₄ tsp. salt
*¹/₄ tsp. **each** freshly*
  ground black pepper
  and crushed red pepper
¹/₃ cup olive oil
6 large cloves garlic,
  minced or pressed
8 oz. dry tagliarini
Grated Parmesan cheese

Peel, seed, and coarsely chop tomatoes. If using canned tomatoes, break up with a spoon. In a bowl, combine tomatoes, water (omit if using canned tomatoes), basil, salt, black pepper, and red pepper; reserve.

Place olive oil and garlic in a 1-quart pan. Cook, stirring occasionally, over medium-low heat until oil bubbles gently and garlic is a light gold. (Do not brown garlic or it will taste bitter.) Add tomato mixture to pan and simmer, uncovered, stirring occasionally, for 5 minutes.

Cook noodles in a large pan of boiling water until al dente, following package directions. Drain noodles, then place in a serving bowl. Pour sauce over noodles, toss gently, then serve. Serve with Parmesan at the table.

Makes 4 to 6 servings

Baked Tomato Spaghetti

Baked Roma-type tomatoes and fresh basil make a savory sauce for spaghetti in this Florentine first course. Long cooking partially dries the tomatoes, intensifying their sweetness.

⌇

PER SERVING: *437 calories, 10 g protein, 55 g carbohydrates, 20 g total fat, 9 mg cholesterol, 51 mg sodium*

PREPARATION TIME: *20 min.*
COOKING TIME: *10 to 12 min.*
BAKING TIME: *55 to 1 hr.*
   10 min.

12 medium-size firm-ripe pear-shaped (Roma-type) tomatoes (about 1³/4 lb.)
Salt and pepper
3 to 6 cloves garlic, minced
¹/2 cup chopped parsley
¹/2 cup olive oil
1 lb. dry spaghetti
2 Tbsp. butter or margarine, at room temperature
¹/2 cup whole fresh basil leaves or 2 Tbsp. dry basil
Grated Parmesan cheese

Cut tomatoes in half lengthwise; set, cut sides up, in a shallow 9- by 13-inch baking pan or dish. Sprinkle lightly with salt and pepper. Mix garlic, ¹/4 cup of the parsley, and 2 tablespoons of the oil; pat mixture over cut sides of tomatoes. Drizzle with 2 tablespoons more oil. Bake, uncovered, in a 425° oven until browned on top (55 to 70 minutes; pan juices may become very dark).

When tomatoes are almost done, in a 6- to 8-quart pan, cook spaghetti in 4 quarts boiling water until al dente (10 to 12 minutes, or according to package directions).

Meanwhile, peel 4 of the tomato halves and place in a warm serving bowl with the butter, remaining parsley, remaining ¹/4 cup oil, and basil; coarsely mash.

Drain spaghetti; add to tomato mixture and mix lightly, using 2 forks. Add remaining baked tomato halves and pan juices. Mix gently; season to taste with salt and pepper. Serve with cheese, if desired.

Makes 6 to 8 first-course servings

ROBUST MEALS

Linguine with Lentils

*Lentils and Swiss chard, flavored in a spicy broth,
combine with linguine and creamy Neufchâtel cheese
for a satisfying main dish.*

⌒

PER SERVING: *467 calories, 21 g protein, 68 g carbohydrates, 13 g total fat, 22 mg cholesterol, 743 mg sodium*

PREPARATION TIME: *15 min.*
COOKING TIME: *55 min.*

*3 vegetable bouillon cubes,
   dissolved in 3 cups
   boiling water*
*1 cup lentils, rinsed
   and drained*
1 tsp. cumin seeds
*1 lb. Swiss chard,
   well rinsed*
2 Tbsp. olive oil
1 large onion, chopped
*2 cloves garlic, minced
   or pressed*
*½ tsp. crushed red
   pepper flakes*
12 oz. dry linguine
*6 oz. Neufchâtel
   cheese, diced*
Salt and pepper

In a 5- to 6-quart pan, bring 2 cups of the bouillon
to a boil over high heat. Add lentils and cumin seeds.
Reduce heat, cover, and simmer until lentils are tender (about 30 minutes). Drain and pour into a bowl.

Cut off and discard coarse stem ends of chard; cut
stems and leaves crosswise into ¼-inch-wide strips.

To lentil pan, add oil, chard stems, onion, garlic,
and red pepper flakes. Cook over medium heat, stirring often, until onion is lightly browned (about 15
minutes). Add chard leaves; cook, stirring, until limp
(about 3 minutes). Add lentils and 1 cup bouillon;
cook, uncovered, until hot (about 3 minutes).

Meanwhile, cook pasta in another large pan of
boiling water until al dente. Drain and pour into
a wide bowl. Add lentil mixture and cheese; mix
lightly to blend. Season with salt and pepper.

Makes 6 servings

Vegetable Lasagne

*This meatless lasagne is layered with a rich
tomato sauce, and the goodness of tofu, spinach,
carrots, and zucchini.*

⁓

PER SERVING: *459 calories, 31 g protein, 54 g carbohydrates, 16 g total fat, 28 mg cholesterol, 495 mg sodium*

PREPARATION TIME: *45 min.*
BAKING TIME: *25 min.*

*1 lb. firm tofu
8 oz. dry lasagne noodles
1 lb. carrots, thinly sliced
1 lb. zucchini, thinly sliced
1 Tbsp. salad oil
1 large onion, chopped
1 lb. mushrooms, sliced
1 tsp. **each** dry basil, thyme,
  and oregano leaves
2 cans (15 oz. each) no-
  salt-added tomato sauce
1 can (6 oz.) tomato paste
2 packages (10 oz. each)
  frozen chopped spinach,
  thawed and squeezed dry
1 cup part-skim ricotta
2 cups (8 oz.) shredded
  part-skim mozzarella
¼ cup grated Parmesan*

In a 5- to 6-quart pan, cook pasta in 3 quarts boiling water until al dente (about 10 minutes). Lift out pasta, rinse and drain; set aside. Add carrots to pan. After 6 minutes add zucchini; cook until vegetables are tender-crisp. Drain; set aside.

Heat oil in pan over medium-high heat. Add coarse chunks of tofu (patted dry), onion, mushrooms, and herbs. Cook, stirring, until liquid has evaporated. Stir in tomato sauce and tomato paste. Remove from heat; set aside.

In a bowl, mix spinach and ricotta; set aside. Spread a third of the sauce in a 9- by 13-inch baking pan. Top with half the noodles, then half each carrots, zucchini, spinach, and mozzarella. Repeat, ending with sauce. Sprinkle top with Parmesan.

Set pan on baking sheet. Bake in a 400° oven for about 25 minutes). Let stand 5 minutes.

Makes 8 servings

Fettuccine Alfredo

*Immortalized by Alfredo's restaurant in Rome,
this is the recipe everyone thinks of when you say "fettuccine."
It is very rich and so good!*

∞

PER SERVING: *619 calories, 15 g protein, 35 g carbohydrates, 47 g total fat, 192 mg cholesterol, 649 mg sodium*

PREPARATION TIME: *5 min.*
COOKING TIME: *10 min.*

*8 oz. dry medium-
    wide noodles*
6 Tbsp. butter or margarine
1½ cups whipping cream
*1 cup (3 oz.) grated
    Parmesan cheese*
Salt and pepper
Whole or ground nutmeg

Cook noodles in a large pan of boiling salted water until al dente, following package directions. Drain.

While noodles are cooking, melt butter in a wide frying pan over high heat until butter is lightly browned. Add ½ cup of the cream and boil rapidly until slightly thickened. Reduce heat to medium. Add noodles to sauce and toss gently. Then add half the cheese and ½ cup of remaining cream. Toss gently; repeat with remaining cheese and cream; toss again.

Season with salt and pepper to taste and grate nutmeg generously over noodles (or use about ⅛ teaspoon ground nutmeg). Serve immediately.

Makes 4 to 6 first-course servings

Ham & Mushroom Spaghetti

*Here's a family-pleasing spaghetti main dish.
It's lightly seasoned, and it has just enough cream to give it
a velvet-rich texture.*

PER SERVING: *472 calories, 25 g protein, 38 g carbohydrates, 25 g total fat, 92 mg cholesterol, 1450 mg sodium*

PREPARATION TIME: *15 min.*
COOKING TIME: *12 min.*

3 Tbsp. butter or margarine
*1/2 lb. mushrooms, thinly
sliced*
*1/2 lb. thinly sliced cooked
ham, cut into thin strips*
3/4 cup canned tomato juice
1/2 tsp. rubbed sage
1/8 tsp. ground nutmeg
1/3 cup whipping cream
1/4 cup chopped parsley
*1/2 cup grated Parmesan
cheese*
*6 oz. dry spaghetti
or vermicelli*

In a large frying pan over medium-high heat, melt butter. Add mushrooms and cook, stirring occasionally, until juices evaporate and mushrooms are lightly browned. Add ham, tomato juice, sage, nutmeg, and cream. Boil, uncovered, over high heat, stirring occasionally, until liquid is reduced to about half (about 8 minutes). Stir in parsley and 1 tablespoon of the cheese.

Meanwhile, cook spaghetti in a large pan of boiling salted water until al dente, following package directions; then drain. Return spaghetti to pan, pour sauce over spaghetti, and toss gently. Turn into a serving bowl. Sprinkle with Parmesan at the table.

Makes 4 servings

Fettuccine a Quattro Formaggi

*In this luscious, dish three of the four
cheeses—Fontina, Bel Paese, and Gorgonzola—blend
to make the grand duke of all cheese sauces.*

∽

PER SERVING: *432 calories, 17 g protein, 37 g carbohydrates, 24 g total fat, 110 mg cholesterol, 731 mg sodium*

PREPARATION TIME: *15 min.*
COOKING TIME: *15 min.*

3 Tbsp. butter or margarine
1½ Tbsp. all-purpose flour
⅛ tsp. ground nutmeg
Dash of white pepper
*1 cup half-and-half
  (light cream)*
½ cup chicken broth
*⅓ cup **each** shredded
  Fontina and Bel Paese
  cheeses*
*⅓ cup crumbled
  Gorgonzola cheese*
*8 oz. dry medium-wide
  noodles*
*½ cup grated Parmesan
  cheese*

In a 2-quart pan over medium heat, melt 1½ tablespoons of the butter. Mix in flour, nutmeg, and pepper and cook, stirring, until bubbly. Remove pan from heat and stir in half-and-half and chicken broth. Return to heat and cook, stirring constantly, until it boils and thickens. Mix in Fontina and Bel Paese cheeses; cook, stirring, until cheeses melt and sauce is smooth. Stir in Gorgonzola until blended; place pan over simmering water to keep sauce warm.

Meanwhile, cook noodles in a large pan of boiling salted water until al dente, following package directions. Drain. Toss noodles lightly with remaining 1½ tablespoons butter and the Parmesan cheese. Spoon noodles onto serving plates. Top each serving with an equal amount of hot cheese sauce. Sprinkle with Parmesan cheese.

Makes 4 to 6 servings

Minestrone Genovese

P A S T A

*In Italy, minestrone comes in countless
variations, which can be eaten cool in the summer,
and hot in the winter.*

⌒⌒

PER SERVING: 289 calories, 16 g protein, 35 g carbohydrates, 11 g total fat, 6 mg cholesterol, 1390 mg sodium

PREPARATION TIME: *10 min.*
COOKING TIME: *20 min.*

2 large leeks
1 large red bell pepper
2 large carrots, peeled
*1 lb. (about 4 large) yellow
  crookneck squash*
3 stalks celery, thinly sliced
3 qt. chicken broth
*2 cans (15 oz. each) white
  kidney beans, drained*
4 oz. dry macaroni
*2 cups lightly packed
  fresh basil leaves*
*1 cup grated Parmesan
  cheese*
¼ cup olive oil
2 Tbsp. pine nuts
1 or 2 cloves garlic
*1 package (1 lb.) frozen
  petite peas*
Salt and pepper

Trim root ends and green tops off leeks. Split leeks
in half lengthwise, and rinse thoroughly; thinly slice
leeks crosswise. Stem and seed bell pepper; then cut
bell pepper, carrots, and squash into ½-inch chunks.

In an 8- to 10-quart pan, combine leeks, carrots,
celery, and broth; bring to a boil. Cover and simmer
10 minutes. Add beans, macaroni, squash, and bell
pepper; cover and simmer just until macaroni is
cooked al dente (about 10 minutes).

Meanwhile, in a food processor or blender, purée
basil leaves, Parmesan cheese, olive oil, pine nuts,
and garlic. Add salt to taste. Set the pesto aside.

Add peas to the soup; return the soup to a boil,
then stir in ½ cup pesto. Serve soup hot or cold.
Offer remaining pesto, salt, and pepper to add
to taste.

Makes 10 to 12 servings

Red Hot Macaroni & Cheese

Where is it written
that because a dish is meatless it has to be boring?
Zap those taste buds awake with this dish.

PER SERVING: 607 calories, 22 g protein, 48 g carbohydrates, 36 g total fat, 116 mg cholesterol, 438 mg sodium

PREPARATION TIME: *15 min.*
COOKING TIME: *60 min.*

1 lb. medium-size dry
  macaroni
1/3 cup butter or margarine
1 medium-size onion,
  finely chopped
1/2 cup finely chopped
  celery
1/3 cup all-purpose flour
2 1/4 cups milk
1 cup whipping cream
1 tsp. **each** crushed red
  pepper and
  Worcestershire sauce
4 cups (1 lb.) shredded
  sharp Cheddar cheese
1/2 cup dry white wine
Salt and pepper
1 red bell pepper, cut
  into rings

Cook macaroni in a large pan of boiling water until *al dente*, following package directions; then drain and set aside.

Meanwhile, melt butter in a large frying pan over medium heat. Add onion and celery and cook, stirring occasionally, until tender (about 5 minutes). Stir in flour and cook for 1 minute. Remove pan from heat and gradually stir in milk and cream. Return pan to heat and cook, stirring constantly, until smooth and thick.

Reduce heat and add red pepper, Worcestershire sauce, and 3 cups of the cheese. Stir until cheese melts; add wine. Combine cooked macaroni and cheese sauce; add salt and pepper to taste. Turn into a shallow 3-quart baking dish; arrange bell pepper rings on top, then sprinkle with remaining cheese.

Bake, uncovered, in a 375° oven for 25 to 35 minutes or until bubbly and lightly browned.

Makes 8 to 10 servings

Italian Sausage & Pasta with Basil

*The combination of robust sausages
and green bell peppers at once recalls the boisterous bustle
of an Italian street fair.*

⟨∞⟩

PER SERVING: 562 calories, 25 g protein, 53 g carbohydrates, 28 g total fat, 52 mg cholesterol, 853 mg sodium

PREPARATION TIME: *15 min.*
COOKING TIME: *20 min.*

1 lb. mild Italian sausages,
  casings removed
1 large onion, coarsely
  chopped
1 large green bell pepper,
  seeded and coarsely
  chopped
2 cloves garlic, minced
  or pressed
1 can (14$\frac{1}{2}$ oz. to 1 lb.)
  tomatoes
12 oz. dry vermicelli
  (not coil vermicelli) or
  spaghettini
2 to 3 Tbsp. dry basil
$\frac{1}{4}$ cup chopped parsley
$\frac{3}{4}$ to 1 cup grated
  Parmesan cheese
$\frac{1}{4}$ cup olive oil

Crumble sausages into a large frying pan over medium-high heat. Cook, stirring often, until meat begins to brown. Add onion and bell pepper; continue to cook, stirring, until onion is soft but not brown (about 5 minutes). Spoon off and discard excess fat. Stir in garlic, then tomatoes (break up with a spoon) and their liquid. Bring to a boil; reduce heat and boil gently, uncovered, stirring often, until slightly thickened (about 10 minutes).

Meanwhile, in a 6- to 8-quart pan, cook vermicelli in 4 quarts boiling water until al dente (8 to 10 minutes, or cook according to package directions.) Drain well.

In a warm serving bowl, combine basil, parsley, $\frac{1}{2}$ cup of the cheese, and oil. Add vermicelli and mix lightly, using 2 forks. Top with sausage-tomato sauce. Sprinkle with remaining cheese.

Makes 6 servings

Rotelle with Tomato Sauce

A robust, garlic-and-onion flavored
tomato sauce made with pure butter and olive oil
dresses corkscrew-shaped noodles.

∞

PER SERVING: 555 calories, 10 g protein, 58 g carbohydrates, 32 g total fat, 47 mg cholesterol, 1217 mg sodium

PREPARATION TIME: 10 min.
COOKING TIME: 1 hr. 15 min.

1/4 cup *each* olive oil
  and butter or margarine
3 whole cloves garlic, peeled
1 large onion, thinly sliced
  and separated into rings
5 large tomatoes, peeled,
  seeded, and chopped
1 1/2 tsp. salt
1/4 tsp. pepper
1 tsp. oregano leaves
8 oz. dry rotelle, or other
  spiral-shaped pasta
Grated Parmesan cheese
1/4 lb. mushrooms, sliced
  and sautéed in 2 Tbsp.
  butter (optional)

Heat oil and butter in a large frying pan over medium heat. Add garlic and onion; cook, stirring occasionally, until onion is limp. Remove garlic and add
tomatoes, salt, pepper, and oregano; bring to a boil.
Reduce heat, cover, and simmer, stirring occasionally,
until sauce has thickened (about 1 hour).

Following package directions, cook rotelle in a
large pan of boiling salted water until al dente. Drain
and turn onto a deep platter. Spoon tomato sauce
over rotelle, sprinkle with Parmesan, and top with
sautéed mushrooms, if desired.

Makes 4 servings

Spaghetti Marinara

*You don't have to brown the pork cubes
for this recipe; they simmer to fork-tender succulence
in an herb-seasoned tomato sauce.*

∽

PER SERVING: 564 calories, 37 g protein, 70 g carbohydrates, 15 g total fat, 87 mg cholesterol, 1585 mg sodium

PREPARATION TIME: *15 min.*
COOKING TIME: *1 hr. 30 min.*

2 Tbsp. olive oil
1 onion, finely chopped
1 carrot, finely chopped
1 green pepper
4 cloves minced garlic
1 can (1 lb.) tomato purée
3 cans (8 oz. each)
*   tomato sauce*
1/2 cup dry red wine
2 tsp. salt
1 Tbsp. sugar
1/4 tsp. black pepper
1/8 tsp. cayenne pepper
*1 tsp. **each** dry rosemary,*
*   oregano leaves, dry basil*
1 bay leaf
2 lb. lean boneless pork
*   shoulder, cubed*
1/4 lb. mushrooms, sliced
1 lb. dry spaghetti
Grated Parmesan cheese

Seed and finely chop green pepper. Heat olive oil in a 6- to 8-quart pan over medium heat. Add onion, carrot, green pepper, and garlic; cook until vegetables are tender. Add tomato purée, tomato sauce, red wine, salt, sugar, black pepper, cayenne pepper, rosemary, oregano, basil, bay leaf, and pork shoulder, cut in 1/2-inch cubes. Bring to a boil, reduce heat, cover, and simmer for 1 1/2 hours or until pork is fork-tender. Add mushrooms and simmer, uncovered, for about 10 minutes more. Remove bay leaf.

Cook spaghetti in a large pan of boiling water until al dente, following package directions; drain and toss with grated cheese to taste. Arrange spaghetti on a serving dish, ladle sauce over it, and serve.

Makes 6 to 8 servings

Chicken Vermicelli Carbonara

*Here's a creative lowfat version of an Italian classic.
Chicken stands in for the usual pork; chopped onion, braised and
deglazed in fennel-seasoned broth, adds a rich, browned flavor.*

∞

PER SERVING: *409 calories, 30 g protein, 47 g carbohydrates, 10 g total fat, 91 mg cholesterol, 489 mg sodium*

PREPARATION TIME: *25 min.*
COOKING TIME: *30 min.*

*1 large onion, finely chopped
1/2 tsp. fennel seeds
1 3/4 cups low-sodium
   chicken broth
12 to 14 oz. boneless,
   skinless chicken thighs,
   trimmed of fat and cut
   into 1/2-inch chunks
1 cup finely chopped parsley
3 egg whites
1 egg
12 oz. to 1 lb. dry vermicelli
1 1/2 cups (about 6 oz.) finely
   shredded Parmesan cheese
Salt and freshly ground
   pepper*

In a large frying pan, combine onion, fennel seeds, and 1 cup of broth. Bring to a boil; stir until liquid evaporates and browned bits accumulate. Deglaze pan by adding 2 tablespoons water and stirring to loosen browned bits. Repeat deglazing until onions are golden brown. Add chicken and 2 tablespoons water; continue to cook and deglaze with water until chicken and drippings are brown. Add remaining broth; bring to a boil. Add parsley; keep warm over lowest heat.

In a bowl, blend egg whites and egg; set aside.

Cook vermicelli in 4 quarts boiling water until al dente (8 to 10 minutes, or according to package directions.) Drain. Add pasta to pan; pour eggs over pasta and at once begin lifting and mixing with 2 forks, adding 1 cup of cheese. Pour onto warm platter and mix until broth is absorbed. Season with remaining cheese, salt, and pepper.

Makes 6 to 8 servings

FESTIVE FARE

Penne with Smoked Salmon

*V*odka emphasizes the flavor of a creamy,
*tomato-dotted sauce for silken smoked salmon
and pasta tubes.*

⌒

PER SERVING: *606 calories, 19 g protein, 67 g carbohydrates, 25 g total fat, 63 mg cholesterol, 303 mg sodium*

PREPARATION TIME: *10 min.*
COOKING TIME: *10 to 12 min.*

12 oz. dry penne
2 Tbsp. olive oil
1 small shallot, sliced
4 small pear-shaped
   tomatoes (about 6 oz.),
   peeled, seeded, and
   chopped
²/₃ cup whipping cream
Pinch of ground nutmeg
2 Tbsp. chopped fresh dill
   or ¹/₂ tsp. dry dill weed
¹/₃ cup vodka
4 to 6 oz. sliced smoked
   salmon or lox, cut into
   bite-size strips
Ground white pepper
Fresh dill sprigs

In a 6- to 8-quart pan, cook pasta in 4 quarts boiling water until al dente (10 to 12 minutes, or according to package directions). Drain well.

While pasta is cooking, heat oil in a large frying pan over medium-low heat. Add shallot and cook, stirring often, until soft but not brown (about 3 minutes). Stir in chopped tomatoes, cover, and simmer for 5 minutes. Add cream, nutmeg, chopped dill, and vodka. Increase heat to high and bring to a full boil; boil for 1 minute.

Add pasta to sauce and mix lightly, using 2 spoons, until pasta is well coated. Remove from heat. Add salmon, and mix lightly. Season to taste with white pepper and garnish with dill sprigs.

Makes 4 servings

Linguine
with Morels &
Asparagus

*In a spectacular gathering of gastronomic treasures,
spring asparagus and flavorful morels lend elegance to
golden, creamy pasta.*

∽

PER SERVING: *530 calories, 13 g protein, 41 g carbohydrates, 36 g total fat, 111 mg cholesterol, 274 mg sodium*

SOAKING TIME: *45 min.*
PREPARATION TIME: *10 min.*
COOKING TIME: *12 to 15 min.*

*¹/₂ to 1 cup (¹/₂ to 1 oz.)
dried morel mushrooms*
*12 oz. asparagus, tough
ends snapped off, spears
cut into 1-inch-long pieces*
2 Tbsp. pine nuts
3 Tbsp. butter or margarine
*2 Tbsp. finely chopped
shallot*
1 cup whipping cream
6 oz. dry linguine
*2 Tbsp. 1-inch-long
chive strips*
*1 tsp. chopped fresh thyme
or ¹/₄ tsp. dry thyme leaves*
Salt
*¹/₃ to ¹/₂ cup grated
Parmesan cheese*

Soak mushrooms in a bowl of hot water for 45 minutes. Drain, reserving ¹/₂ cup of the liquid. Cut mushrooms into halves or quarters; pat dry and set aside.

Steam asparagus, covered, on a rack over 1 inch of boiling water for 3 to 4 minutes. Remove from pan.

Stir pine nuts in a large frying pan over medium-low heat until lightly browned (about 3 minutes); remove from pan. Increase heat to medium. Melt butter in pan; add mushrooms and shallot. Cook, stirring often, until mushrooms are lightly browned (4 to 5 minutes). Add ¹/₂ cup mushroom liquid and cream. Increase heat to high, bring mixture to a boil, and boil, stirring often, until liquid is reduced by about a third.

Meanwhile, cook linguine in 3 quarts boiling water until al dente (8 to 10 minutes). Drain well and divide among wide, shallow bowls. To sauce, add chives, thyme, and asparagus; stir just until heated through. Season with salt. Spoon over linguine; sprinkle with pine nuts. Serve with cheese.

Makes 4 first-course servings

Spaghetti with White Clam Sauce

With canned clams in your pantry,
you can make this traditional Italian favorite on a moment's
notice for a festive company meal.

PER SERVING: 577 calories, 23 g protein, 61 g carbohydrates, 27 g total fat, 73 mg cholesterol, 480 mg sodium

PREPARATION TIME: *10 min.*
COOKING TIME: *15 min.*

1/2 cup butter
1/4 cup olive oil
4 cloves garlic, minced
or pressed
3 cans (6 1/2 oz. each)
chopped clams
*1 tsp. **each** oregano leaves*
and dry basil (or 1 Tbsp.
fresh basil)
1/4 tsp. cayenne pepper
1 1/2 cups chopped parsley
1 lb. dry spaghetti or
linguine

In a 2-quart pan over medium-low heat, melt butter in olive oil. Add garlic and cook until golden; do not let garlic burn. Drain the juice from 2 of the cans of clams into butter mixture; reserve juice from the third can for other uses. Add oregano, basil, cayenne pepper, and parsley to pan; simmer for 5 minutes. Add drained clams and heat through.

Meanwhile, following package directions, cook spaghetti in a large pan of boiling salted water until al dente; then drain. Toss clam sauce with spaghetti.

Makes 5 or 6
main-dish servings

Pasta & Sausage in Madeira Cream

*Madeira or sherry mellows the flavor of
Italian sausage, helping the spicy meat blend smoothly
with a mushroom cream sauce.*

∽

PER SERVING: *743 calories, 28 g protein, 57 g carbohydrates, 43 g total fat, 129 mg cholesterol, 870 mg sodium*

PREPARATION TIME: *15 min.*
COOKING TIME: *25 min.*

1 lb. mild Italian sausages,
  casings removed
12 oz. dry bite-size spinach
  rotelle or fusilli
4 oz. mushrooms, sliced
2 large cloves garlic,
  minced or pressed
1/4 cup Madeira or
  dry sherry
1 cup whipping cream
1 tsp. ground white pepper
1/4 tsp. ground nutmeg
1/2 to 3/4 cup grated
  Parmesan cheese

Crumble sausages into a wide frying pan over medium-high heat; cook, stirring often, until well browned (10 to 15 minutes). Lift out sausage and set aside. Discard all but 2 tablespoons of the drippings.

In a 6- to 8-quart pan, cook pasta in 4 quarts boiling water until al dente (about 10 minutes, or according to package directions).

Meanwhile, add mushrooms and garlic to drippings; cook, stirring often, until mushrooms are brown (8 to 10 minutes). Stir in Madeira, scraping up browned bits from pan. Add sausage, cream, white pepper, and nutmeg. Increase heat to high, and boil until large, shiny bubbles form and sauce is slightly thickened (1 to 2 minutes).

Drain pasta and transfer to a warm serving bowl. Top with sausage sauce; mix lightly, using 2 forks. Serve with cheese to add to taste.

Makes 4 to 6 servings

P A S T A

Perciatelli with Mussels Marinara

*The combination of bouncy perciatelli—fat,
hollow strands—and mussels calls for a wide napkin
tucked under the chin.*

∾

PER SERVING: 383 calories, 15 g protein, 51 g carbohydrates, 12 g total fat, 14 mg cholesterol, 528 mg sodium

PREPARATION TIME: *10 min.*
COOKING TIME: *20 to 25 min.*

*1 qt. mussels in the shells
3 Tbsp. olive oil
½ small onion, chopped
1 clove garlic, minced
  or pressed
1 can (about 1 lb.)
  Italian-style tomatoes
½ tsp. oregano leaves
Dash of cayenne pepper
2 Tbsp. chopped parsley
¼ cup dry white wine
8 oz. dry perciatelli or
  thick spaghetti*

Scrub mussels with a stiff brush under running water. With a knife, scrape off the tuft of hairs, which protrudes from one side of the closed shell.

Heat oil in a Dutch oven over medium heat. When oil is hot, add onion and garlic and cook until onion is limp. Add tomatoes and their liquid (break up with a spoon), oregano, cayenne pepper, parsley, and wine. Reduce heat and simmer uncovered for 10 minutes, stirring occasionally. Add mussels and stir to coat with sauce. Cover and simmer just until mussels have opened (5 to 8 minutes). Discard any that don't open.

Cook pasta in a large pan of boiling salted water until al dente, following package directions; then drain. Return pasta to pan, pour over mussels and sauce, and lift and mix gently so all pasta is coated with sauce. Turn into a serving bowl.

Makes 4 servings

Orecchiette with Spinach & Garlic

You might take shallow orecchiette
for diminutive berets, but their Italian name indicates
that they're meant to be seen as little ears.

∽

PER SERVING: *364 calories, 12 g protein, 46 g carbohydrates, 15 g total fat, 4 mg cholesterol, 173 mg sodium*

PREPARATION TIME: *20 min.*
COOKING TIME: *15 min.*

2 bunches (about 12 oz.
  each) spinach, rinsed
  well and drained
12 oz. dry orecchiette
  or ruote (wheel-shaped
  pasta)
$^1/_3$ cup olive oil
6 cloves garlic, minced
  or pressed
$^1/_2$ tsp. crushed, dried
  hot red chilies
Salt
$^1/_3$ to $^1/_2$ cup grated
  Parmesan cheese

Remove and discard spinach stems; chop leaves coarsely and set aside.

In a 6- to 8-quart pan, cook orecchiette in 4 quarts boiling water until al dente (12 to 15 minutes, or according to package directions). Just before pasta is done, stir in spinach. Cook, uncovered, stirring to distribute spinach, just until water returns to a full boil. Drain pasta and spinach.

While pasta is cooking, heat oil in a large frying pan over medium heat. Stir in garlic and chiles. Cook, uncovered, until garlic turns opaque (about 2 minutes). Add pasta and spinach to pan; mix lightly, using 2 spoons. Season to taste with salt. Serve with cheese to add to taste.

Makes 6 first-course servings

Farfalle with Grilled Chicken & Pesto Cream

The Italians see these little noodles as butterflies, or farfalle; to others, they may look more like bow ties.

◌◌

PER SERVING: *730 calories, 40 g protein, 47 g carbohydrates, 42 g total fat, 165 mg cholesterol, 346 mg sodium*

PREPARATION TIME: *15 min.*
COOKING TIME: *15 to 20 min.*

2 Tbsp. pine nuts
1 clove garlic, chopped
1/2 cup **each** parsley sprigs
  and fresh basil leaves
2 Tbsp. coarsely chopped
  fresh mint leaves
1 green onion, thinly sliced
1/8 tsp. pepper
Pinch of ground nutmeg
3 Tbsp. olive oil
1/4 cup butter, melted
2 whole chicken breasts
  (about 1 lb. each),
  skinned, boned, and split
10 oz. dry farfalle
1/4 cup dry white wine
1 cup whipping cream
Salt
2 Tbsp. chopped roasted
  red pepper
1/2 cup grated Parmesan

Stir pine nuts in a small frying pan over medium-low heat until lightly browned (about 3 minutes). In a blender, purée 1 tablespoon pine nuts, garlic, parsley, basil, mint, green onion, pepper, nutmeg, 2 tablespoons olive oil, and butter; set pesto aside.

Rinse chicken and pat dry. Brush all sides with oil. Place a ridged cooktop grill pan over medium heat. Place chicken on hot pan and cook, turning once, until well browned on outside and no longer pink in center (10 minutes *total*). Cut into 1/2-inch-wide strips.

Meanwhile, cook pasta in 3 quarts boiling water until al dente (about 10 minutes). Drain, and set aside.

In a large frying pan, combine pesto and wine. Cook over medium heat, stirring, until bubbly (about 2 minutes). Stir in cream and bring to a full rolling boil, stirring often. Season with salt, then add roasted pepper, pasta, and chicken; mix lightly, using 2 spoons. Sprinkle mixture with 1 tablespoon pine nuts. Sprinkle with Parmesan at the table.

Makes 4 to 6 servings

Ginger Linguine with Smoked Scallops

The woodsy flavor of oven-smoked scallops blends hauntingly with fresh ginger and cream in this rich sauce for linguine.

∽

PER SERVING: *528 calories, 28 g protein, 49 g carbohydrates, 24 g total fat, 119 mg cholesterol, 250 mg sodium*

PREPARATION TIME: *5 min.*
SMOKING TIME: *12 to 15 min.*
COOKING TIME: *10 to 12 min.*

1 lb. scallops, rinsed and patted dry
3 Tbsp. liquid smoke
8 oz. dry linguine
*1¹/2 Tbsp. **each** tarragon wine vinegar and grated fresh ginger*
¹/4 cup thinly sliced shallots
1 cup whipping cream
¹/2 cup dry white wine
1 tsp. Dijon mustard
Chopped parsley

If scallops are large, cut them into bite-size pieces. Pour liquid smoke into a 5- to 6-quart pan with ovenproof handles. Set a perforated or wire rack in pan. Arrange scallops in a single layer on rack and cover tightly. Bake in a 350° oven until scallops are opaque throughout (12 to 15 minutes); cut to test.

While scallops are smoking, in another 5- to 6-quart pan, cook linguine in 3 quarts boiling water until al dente (8 to 10 minutes, or according to package directions). Drain well.

Combine vinegar, ginger, and shallots in a wide frying pan over high heat; cook until vinegar has evaporated (about 1 minute). Add cream, wine, and mustard. Bring to a full boil; then boil, uncovered, stirring often, until sauce is reduced to 1¹/4 cups. Reduce heat to medium; add scallops and mix lightly until heated through (1 to 2 minutes). Add linguine; mix lightly, using 2 spoons. Sprinkle with parsley.

Makes 4 servings

Angel Hair Pasta with Crab

Capelli d'angeli, or angel hair, pasta casts a spell in this recipe—with fresh crab, white wine, lemon, and tomato—and the initial enthusiasm is completely justified. What's more, this dish is quick to cook.

∽

PER SERVING: 468 calories, 20 g protein, 47 g carbohydrates, 21 g total fat, 72 mg cholesterol, 425 mg sodium

PREPARATION TIME: *15 min.*
COOKING TIME: *10 to 15 min.*

*8 oz. dry capelli d'angeli
  or capellini
2 Tbsp. butter or margarine
¹/₄ cup olive oil
¹/₂ cup sliced green onions
1 clove garlic, minced
  or pressed
2 medium-size ripe
  tomatoes, peeled, seeded,
  and chopped
¹/₄ cup dry white wine
1 Tbsp. lemon juice
¹/₂ lb. cooked crab, flaked
¹/₄ cup chopped fresh
  parsley
Salt and pepper*

Cook noodles in a large pan of boiling salted water until al dente, following package directions. Drain well and place on a warm platter. Keep warm.

Meanwhile, place butter and oil in a large frying pan over medium heat. When butter is melted, add green onions, garlic, tomatoes, and wine. Cook, stirring, until mixture boils. Adjust heat so mixture boils gently, and cook for 2 minutes. Mix in lemon juice, crab, and parsley. Cook, stirring, just until crab is heated through. Season to taste with salt and pepper. Spoon sauce over pasta. Lift and mix pasta gently, then serve.

Makes 4 servings

Shrimp Conchiglie

Following the Northern Italian tradition that avoids tomato sauce, shrimp conchiglie is a delicately sauced combination of seafood

∞

PER SERVING: *405 calories, 17 g protein, 37 g carbohydrates, 21 g total fat, 148 mg cholesterol, 480 mg sodium*

PREPARATION TIME: *10 min.*
COOKING TIME: *15 min.*

*12 oz. dry conchiglie
  or other medium-size
  shell-shaped pasta*
³/₄ cup butter
1¹/₂ tsp. dry basil
1 Tbsp. minced parsley
³/₄ lb. small cooked shrimp
1 tsp. dry sherry
Salt
Grated Parmesan cheese

Following package directions, cook pasta in a large pan of boiling salted water until al dente (about 8 to 10 minutes). Drain well and turn onto a platter; keep warm.

Meanwhile, melt butter in a small pan over low heat. Add basil and parsley to pan, and heat until bubbly. Add shrimp and sherry, simmering until shrimp are opaque throughout (3 to 4 minutes).

Pour shrimp sauce over cooked pasta and sprinkle with salt and Parmesan cheese to taste. Mix gently and serve.

Makes 6 to 8 servings

Tricolor Pasta with Brandied Shrimp

Thin strands of golden, spinach-green, and rosy tomato-flavored linguine mingle vividly with juicy shrimp flamed in a buttery sauce with sliced fresh mushrooms.

∽

PER SERVING: 518 calories, 28 g protein, 52 g carbohydrates, 20 g total fat, 186 mg cholesterol, 387 mg sodium

PREPARATION TIME: *30 min.*
COOKING TIME: *10 min.*

6 Tbsp. butter or margarine
2 Tbsp. lemon juice
1 lb. medium-size raw
  shrimp (35 to 45 per lb.),
  shelled, deveined,
  and butterflied
1/4 cup brandy
1/2 tsp. **each** dry tarragon
  and Worcestershire sauce
1/4 tsp. ground ginger
1 tsp. Dijon mustard
6 oz. mushrooms,
  thinly sliced
9 oz. fresh tricolor linguine
Chopped parsley

Melt 3 tablespoons of the butter in a large frying pan over medium heat. Stir in lemon juice; cook, stirring, until bubbly. Add shrimp and cook, stirring often, until opaque throughout (3 to 4 minutes).

Heat brandy in a small pan over low heat until barely warm to the touch. Carefully pour brandy over shrimp; ignite at once. Stir gently until flames are gone. Lift out shrimp and set aside.

To drippings in pan, add remaining butter, tarragon, Worcestershire sauce, ginger, and mustard. Stir until well combined. Increase heat to medium-high. Add mushrooms and cook, stirring, until lightly browned. Return shrimp to pan and stir lightly until heated through (about 1 minute). Season with salt.

Meanwhile, cook linguine in 3 quarts boiling water until al dente (about 4 minutes). Drain well. Divide pasta among 4 dinner plates, then spoon shrimp sauce over pasta. Garnish with parsley.

Makes 4 servings

Chicken in Port Cream
with Fettuccine

An unusual combination of ingredients produces decidedly elegant results in this simple-to-make dish.

∞

PER SERVING: *649 calories, 42 g protein, 39 g carbohydrates, 31 g total fat, 219 mg cholesterol, 199 mg sodium*

SOAKING TIME: *1 hr.*
PREPARATION TIME: *3 to 5 min.*
COOKING TIME: *30 min.*

3/4 cup dried tomatoes
(not packed in oil)
3 whole chicken breasts
(about 1 lb. each),
skinned, boned, and split
3 Tbsp. butter or margarine
1 cup port
1 1/2 cups whipping cream
8 oz. dry fettuccine
Salt and pepper
Fresh tarragon sprigs

Soak tomatoes in warm water to cover until soft (about 1 hour). Drain, chop coarsely, and set aside.

Rinse chicken; pat dry. Melt butter in a wide frying pan over medium-high heat. Add chicken and cook, turning once, until well browned on outside and no longer pink in center (about 10 minutes total). Lift out chicken and keep warm.

To pan drippings, add port and cream. Increase heat to high and bring to a boil; boil, uncovered, stirring occasionally, until large, shiny bubbles form (10 to 15 minutes). Meanwhile, cook fettuccine in 3 quarts boiling water until al dente (8 to 10 minutes, or according to package directions).

While pasta is cooking, mix tomatoes, chicken, and any chicken juices into cream mixture; season to taste with salt and pepper.

Drain fettuccine; transfer to a warm deep platter. Top with chicken mixture; garnish with tarragon.

Makes 6 servings

Index

Angel hair pasta with crab, 59
Asparagus and morels, with linguine, 48-49

Baked tomato spaghetti, 28-29
Basil and tomatoes, with farfalle, 12-13
Basil with Italian sausage and pasta, 41

Cheese and macaroni, red hot, 40
Cheese (formaggi), fettucine a quattro, 36-37
Chicken and pesto cream, with farfalle, 56-57
Chicken in port cream with fettuccine, 62-63
Chicken vermicelli carbonara, 44-45
Clam sauce, white, with spaghetti, 50
Conchiglie, shrimp, 60
Cool pasta shells with scallops, 22-23
Crab, with angel hair pasta, 59

Farfalle with grilled chicken and pesto cream, 56-57
Farfalle with tomatoes and basil, 12-13
Fettuccine, with chicken in port cream, 62-63
Fettuccine Alfredo, 34
Fettuccine and parsley pesto grilled vegetables, 24-25
Fettuccine a quattro formaggi, 36-37
Fettuccine with pine nut-butter sauce, 20-21

Garlic and spinach, with orecchiette, 54-55
Garlic sauce, with tagliarini, 27
Ginger linguine with smoked scallops, 58
Green noodles with zucchini sauce, 26

Ham and mushroom spaghetti, 35

Italian sausage and pasta with basil, 41

Lentils, with linguine, 30-31

Linguine, ginger, with smoked scallops, 58
Linguine with lentils, 30-31
Linguine with morels and asparagus, 48-49
Linguine with prosciutto and olives, 16-17

Macaroni and cheese, red hot, 40
Madeira cream, pasta and sausage in, 51
Marinara, spaghetti, 43
Midsummer pasta, 19
Minestrone Genovese, 38-39
Morels and asparagus, with linguine, 48-49
Mushroom and ham spaghetti, 35
Mussels, with perciatelli, 52-53

Olives and prosciutto, with linguine, 16-17
Orecchiette with spinach and garlic, 54-55

Parsley-lemon pesto, with pasta, 14-15
Parsley pesto grilled vegetables and fettuccine, 24-25
Pasta, peppery, 18
Pasta, types of, 4-5
Pasta and sausage in Madeira cream, 51
Pasta making techniques, 8-11
Pasta with parsley-lemon pesto, 14-15
Pasta with pine nut-butter sauce, 20-21
Penne with smoked salmon, 46
Peppery pasta, 18
Perciatelli with mussels, 52-53
Pesto, 39
Pesto, parsley, with grilled vegetables and fettuccine, 24-25
Pesto, parsley-lemon, with pasta, 14-15
Pesto cream and grilled chicken, with farfalle, 56-57

Pine nut-butter sauce, with pasta, 20-21
Port cream, chicken in, with fettucine, 62-63
Prosciutto and olives, with linguine, 16-17

Red hot macaroni and cheese, 40
Rotelle with tomato sauce, 42

Salmon, smoked, with penne, 46
Sausage, Italian, and pasta with basil, 41
Sausage and pasta in Madeira cream, 51
Scallops, smoked, with ginger linguine, 58
Scallops, with cool pasta shells, 22-23
Shrimp, brandied, with tricolor pasta, 61
Shrimp conchiglie, 60
Smoked salmon, with penne, 46-47
Smoked scallops, with ginger linguine, 58
Spaghetti, baked tomato, 28-29
Spaghetti, ham and mushroom, 35
Spaghetti Marinara, 43
Spaghetti with white clam sauce, 50
Spinach and garlic, with orecchiette, 54-55

Tagliarini with garlic sauce, 27
Tomatoes and basil, with farfalle, 12-13
Tomato sauce, with rotelle, 42
Tomato spaghetti, baked, 28-29
Tricolor pasta with brandied shrimp, 61

Vegetable lasagne, 32-33
Vegetables, parsley pesto grilled, with fettucine, 24-25
Vermicelli carbonara, chicken, 44-45

Zucchini sauce, with green noodles, 26